PREFACE

Terrace Hill, the Iowa Governor's Residence and a National Historic Landmark, observes its 150th anniversary in 2019. This book is a celebration of that milestone. Completed in 1869, Terrace Hill has intrigued and inspired the public since the first guests walked through its doors for the housewarming party of Arathusa and Benjamin Franklin Allen on January 29, 1869.

In these pages, you will learn about the history of Terrace Hill, the first two families to live there and how it became the residence for Iowa's governors and a public landmark. There are two existing sets of historic black and white photographs of Terrace Hill that include a comprehensive tour of the interior rooms, the exterior and the grounds. The first set is from 1899 and the second set is from 1913. This book serves not only as a photographic tour of the residence, but also as a striking comparison of "before and after" photographs, with present-day, color photographs taken by Des Moines photography team, Gary and Kathleen Hoard. Look closely at the photographs, as you will notice countless similarities and differences; a delightful way to recognize the remarkable amount of work done to restore the property and to see the transition of Terrace Hill from a private home into the Iowa Governor's Residence and a public landmark.

◀ South Lawn, c. 1978

TABLE OF CONTENTS

◀ South Lawn Fountain

THE HISTORY 1
    The Allen Era 3
    The Construction of Terrace Hill 5
    The Hubbell Era 7
    The Iowa Governor's Residence and National Historic Landmark 9
    Iowa History Timeline 10

THE EXTERIOR 13
    North Exterior 14
    East Exterior 16
    South Exterior 18
    West Exterior 20

THE INTERIOR 23
    Drawing Room 24
    Reception Room 26
    Music Room 28
    Dining Room 30
    Main Hall 32
    East Hall 34
    Sitting Room 36
    Library 38
    Grand Staircase 40
    Northwest Bedroom 42
    Northeast Bedroom 44
    Southwest Bedroom 46
    Southeast Bedroom 48
    Third Floor Residence 50

THE GROUNDS 53
    Pool 54
    Carriage House 56
    Gardens 58

THE FUTURE OF TERRACE HILL 65

THE HISTORY

Terrace Hill is an architectural marvel that was completed in 1869 in the developing, fast-growing community of Des Moines. It displays not one, but two elaborately mansarded towers, as well as projections, bays, balconies, lambrequined canopies and columned porches on every front, making the house truly unique. Terrace Hill also has the advantage of a superb location. Perched high above the Raccoon River on its "terraced hill," it commands expansive views in every direction.

Benjamin Franklin Allen and Frederick Marion Hubbell were two teenagers who "went west" to a small, rugged frontier outpost called Fort Des Moines. Their lives later intertwined with one another and with the history of Terrace Hill and Iowa. Benjamin Franklin Allen built Terrace Hill, and Frederick Marion Hubbell and his descendants lived in Terrace Hill for over 70 years. The last Hubbell in residence left Terrace Hill in 1957, whereupon it remained vacant and unused, leaving its fate and ultimate disposition uncertain. In 1971, slightly over a century after its completion, the Hubbell heirs donated Terrace Hill to the state of Iowa, and the latest period in its long and colorful history began.

◀ Grand Staircase and Stained Glass Window

Benjamin Franklin Allen

Northeast Exterior, 1873

THE ALLEN ERA
BENJAMIN FRANKLIN ALLEN
(1829 - 1914)

Fort Des Moines, an Army outpost at the confluence of the Des Moines and Raccoon rivers, was established by Captain James Allen in 1843. Captain Allen engaged in a variety of entrepreneurial ventures while at Fort Des Moines, and, upon his death in 1846, left a sizeable inheritance to his nephew, Benjamin. Benjamin Franklin Allen was born in 1829 and found himself with considerable wealth by the time he moved to Fort Des Moines in 1848 at the age of 19. One of the pioneer settlers of Des Moines, Allen became Iowa's first millionaire and the builder of Terrace Hill.

Allen established himself as a merchant and began widening his business interests. He started a steam sawmill near town and also opened a general store. In 1854, Allen married Arathusa West, the daughter of a respected Fort Des Moines pioneer. In 1855, Allen began his career as a banker and real estate operator, acquiring 34 acres of land that included the future site of Terrace Hill.

In 1857, the same year Fort Des Moines changed its name to the City of Des Moines, Allen became one of the directors of the State Bank of Iowa. Allen soon acquired a controlling interest in the Bank of Nebraska, which he managed from his private banking house in Des Moines. During the Panic of 1857, Allen kept many local businesses afloat by endorsing promissory notes guaranteeing he would pay their debts. By 1860, Allen had been instrumental in transforming Des Moines from a rustic settlement of 200 people into a town of nearly 4,000. In 1867, Allen became one of the directors and a major stockholder of the Chicago Rock Island and Pacific Railroad. He bought up property along the proposed route west to the Missouri River, established a land company, plotted town sites and stations along the route and sold them at a sizeable profit.

Between 1866 and 1869, the Allens built Iowa's most-prized home, Terrace Hill. On January 29, 1869, they hosted a lavish housewarming with 700 guests in attendance, to celebrate their 15th wedding anniversary. However, in May 1873, Allen made a move which hastened his spectacular downfall. In an effort to pay off his already looming debt, he purchased controlling interest in the Cook County National Bank in Chicago and was elected president. Despite Allen's efforts to guarantee the bank by relying on his personal fortune, the bank crashed in January 1875, taking Allen with it. Litigation involving the liquidation of Allen's estate dragged on until the mid-1880s. Although the majority of Allen's assets were sold after he went bankrupt in 1875, he managed to retain possession of Terrace Hill and eight acres of immediate grounds until 1884, when Frederick M. Hubbell purchased the property.

Northeast Exterior, 1899

THE CONSTRUCTION
OF TERRACE HILL
(1866 - 1869)

The construction of Terrace Hill began in 1866 at the height of Allen's fortune. In October 1866, a local newspaper announced the employment of workers to prepare a 29-acre site for Allen's new home. It described "a country residence in modern French design with a mansard roof." Another early newspaper source referred to a "fairy-land castle with towers and turrets." The 29-acre site began at approximately 17th Street on the east, running west to 29th Street. The Raccoon River was the southern border and present-day Grand Avenue was the northern border. Allen selected Chicago architect William W. Boyington to design Terrace Hill. Additionally, Job T. Elletson, a landscape gardener from England, was hired to design the grass-plats, flower banks, vineyards and orchards with gravelled walks and drives throughout.

William W. Boyington, born on July 22, 1818, in Massachusetts, trained first as a carpenter, then as an architect and an engineer. Professionally, Boyington varied his designs from modest cottages to elaborate office and commercial buildings. He was one of the few prominent architects in Chicago before the disastrous Great Chicago Fire of 1871. The Chicago Water Tower (1869) is a rare survivor that still stands today. As an architect without a distinct personal style, Boyington supplied his clients with fashionable designs and was especially fond of the French Second Empire style.

Boyington's plans for Terrace Hill were completed in the spring of 1867. An April 1867 account in the *Iowa State Register* promised, "B.F. Allen's residence will be built and his grounds fitted up immediately." Allen's villa would sit on a terraced site 400 feet off the road. The plans also included a carriage house, an ice house and a self-regulating windmill to pump water from the Raccoon River.

Once completed in 1869, Terrace Hill's floor plan was nearly the same on all four levels. The third floor housed the live-in staff, with their rooms accessed from the large central hall. The basement contained the kitchen, laundry facilities, drying and airing rooms, storerooms, the servants' dining hall and a vault. The first and second floors were decorated in current styles, with carpets, curtains and custom designed furniture acquired from New York. The four marble mantels on the first floor were designed and built by Sherman Cole and Company of Chicago. The grand staircase was built by the local firm, Foster Brothers. Railroads reached Des Moines in 1867 (in large part due to Allen), which aided construction enormously. Allen's accounting during Terrace Hill's construction was scant, but the total cost of the project was estimated between $250,000 and $300,000.

Frederick Marion Hubbell

North Exterior, 1913

THE HUBBELL ERA
FREDERICK MARION HUBBELL
(1839 - 1930)

Frederick Marion (F.M.) Hubbell purchased Terrace Hill in May 1884 for $60,000, approximately one-fifth of what it cost Allen to build the house in 1869. Hubbell came to Fort Des Moines from Connecticut in 1855 at the age of 16. His rise to fame and fortune was equally as phenomenal as Allen's and considerably more lasting. He began as a clerk in the United States land office, securing the job the day after his arrival in Fort Des Moines. A self-taught lawyer, Hubbell became a partner in the law firm of Casady & Polk, later known as Polk & Hubbell, in 1862. In 1866, Polk and Hubbell financed the building of the first streetcar in Des Moines. Three years later they organized a company to continue construction of the Iowa and Minneapolis narrow gauge railroad to Ames. In 1871, Polk and Hubbell established the waterworks for Des Moines, and Hubbell held the controlling interest in the company until 1919 when the city purchased the system. The Equitable Life Insurance Company was founded in 1867, with Hubbell as its first secretary. He was elected president in 1888 and remained at the helm until 1907 when he became chairman of the board.

Hubbell married Frances Cooper in 1863. They had three children: Frederick Cooper Hubbell (born in 1864), Beulah Cooper Hubbell (born in 1874), and Grover Cooper Hubbell (born in 1883). Beulah married Count Carl Axel Wachtmeister, a Swedish diplomat, in 1899. They met in Chicago where he worked for the Swedish-Norwegian consulate. Their wedding was held in the drawing room at Terrace Hill, providing the family with international recognition.

Hubbell was extremely fond of Terrace Hill, and it received exquisite care in his hands. Soon after the Hubbells moved in, mechanical systems were updated, plumbing was modernized and a central heating plant was installed near the carriage house to update the original heating system. Hubbell created a trust in 1903 to protect his assets, including Terrace Hill. Under the terms of this document, the possession of the house passed to the eldest male heir.

The Hubbells celebrated their 61st wedding anniversary with a party at Terrace Hill in 1924, despite Frances' decreasing health. Frances died later that year. After Frances' death, Grover Hubbell, the Hubbells' second son, and his family moved into the house. Grover initiated extensive renovations: an elevator was installed in the former music room, the heating plant was moved into the basement and the house was structurally stabilized and electrified. Modifications were made to the grounds as well. A swimming pool was added east of the house, and a pergola was installed in the formal garden. The bill for this work came to over $50,000.

F.M. lived in Terrace Hill until his death in 1930. At that time, the eldest male heir, Frederick Cooper, chose not to take up residence in the home. Grover and his family continued living in Terrace Hill until Grover's death in 1956. Grover's widow, Anna, moved out of Terrace Hill in 1957, leaving Terrace Hill's future in doubt for many years.

North Lawn, Present Day

THE IOWA GOVERNOR'S RESIDENCE
AND NATIONAL HISTORIC LANDMARK

In its 150-year history, the future of Terrace Hill has been in serious doubt twice. The first instance was after Allen's bankruptcy in 1875; initially, it seemed that Allen might lose the home. The second instance was after Grover Hubbell's death in 1956. With a caretaker living in the basement, the Hubbell Trust managed the property for the next 15 years, paying for insurance, taxes and maintenance. In 1957, the possibility of the state acquiring Terrace Hill emerged. However, the Hubbell Trust barred selling the house, and, at the time, the state did not have a distinct purpose for Terrace Hill.

No official state residence was provided for Iowa's governors from 1846 to 1947, except from 1917 to 1921 when a home at 1027 Des Moines Street was provided for Governor Harding. In 1947, the Georgian Colonial home at 2900 Grand Avenue was purchased as the governor's residence for $27,200. Former governors that lived at 2900 Grand Avenue with their families include: Leo Hoegh, Herschel Loveless, Norman Erbe, Howard Hughes, and Robert Ray. By 1970, a more spacious home was required for the governor's residence, and interest in Terrace Hill reemerged. This time, an agreement with the Hubbell family was reached: they would donate the property to the state by modifying the Hubbell Trust. Once accomplished, the Iowa legislature agreed to accept their generous gift.

In 1971, Governor Ray appointed the 35-member Terrace Hill Planning Commission, which was tasked with determining Terrace Hill's future. Several options were considered: establishing Terrace Hill as a "house museum," or building a new governor's residence on Terrace Hill's eight-acre grounds and using the house for state functions. Eventually, a plan was determined whereby the first family would live on the third floor. The first and second floors would be open for tours and would also be used for official functions. Two of the second-floor bedrooms would be converted into an office for the first spouse, as well as a home office for the governor. The remaining two bedrooms would be used, as needed, for overnight visits by dignitaries and other guests of the first family. In 1976, Governor Ray and his family moved into Terrace Hill, and the house opened for public tours in 1978.

Terrace Hill was designated as a National Historic Landmark in 2003. The prominence of its first two owners and its design as an exceptional example of the French Second Empire style, by noted nineteenth century architect William W. Boyington, contributed to this designation.

Today, Terrace Hill is governed by the Terrace Hill Commission, a nine-member board appointed by the governor. Additional support comes from one organization, the Terrace Hill Partnership, a 501(c) 3 non-profit group that raises funds to preserve and enhance the property and programs of Terrace Hill. They are also active in developing events for the benefit of Terrace Hill.

IOWA HISTORY
TIMELINE

1803 · Napoleon sells all of the Louisiana territory (including Iowa) to the United States

1838 · Territory of Iowa created

1839 · The first decision by the (Territory of) Iowa Supreme Court frees a black slave named Ralph

1843 · May 20, Captain James Allen arrives by boat at the site of the new "Fort Raccoon," however the name is rejected by the War Department and changed to "Fort Des Moines"

1845 · October, Central Iowa opens for settlement

1846 · January, Polk County established
· December 28, Iowa becomes the 29th state of the Union

1848 · Benjamin Franklin Allen arrives in Fort Des Moines

1851 · The town of Fort Des Moines incorporated

1855 · Frederick Marion Hubbell arrives in Fort Des Moines

1857 · February 16, Fort Des Moines becomes the City of Des Moines
· The state capital moves from Iowa City to Des Moines

1861 · Civil War begins

1864 · A local gas plant built for gas lighting

1865 · The Union prevails and the Civil War ends

1866 · The first railroad arrives in Des Moines
· The library is charted as the Public Library of Des Moines
· Allen begins construction on Terrace Hill

1867 · Equitable Life Insurance Company founded

1868 · Iowa Supreme Court decides in Clark v. Board of School Directors ruling that a racially segregated "separate but equal" school has no place in Iowa

1869 · January 29, B. F. and Aarthusa Allen celebrate their 15th wedding anniversary at Terrace Hill
· Iowa becomes the first state in the union to admit women to the practice of law

1871 · Construction begins on the new State Capitol (completed 1886)

1873 · Iowa Supreme Court rules against racial discrimination in public accommodations (91 years before the U. S. Supreme Court reaches the same decision)

1876 · The nation celebrates its centennial

1878 · The first telephones used in Des Moines

1881 · Drake University established

1882 · Des Moines paves some city streets with cedar blocks

1884 · F. M. Hubbell purchases Terrace Hill
- Kindergarten becomes a part of the Des Moines Schools, becoming the second city in the U. S. to make it a part of the curriculum (St. Louis is the first)

1887 · The first electric automobile is made in Des Moines by William Morris

1897 · The first electric lights come to Des Moines

1900 · Census figures give Des Moines 62,000 inhabitants and the state population exceeds two million people

1930 · Iowan Grant Wood paints *American Gothic*

1942 · The Atanasoff-Berry Computer is completed at Iowa State College (now Iowa State University)

1971 · Hubbell family gifts Terrace Hill to the state of Iowa

1972 · Iowa holds initial "first-in-nation" caucus

2003 · Terrace Hill is designated as a National Historic Landmark

2009 · April 3, same sex marriage legally recognized in state of Iowa, nine years before nationwide legalization

2014 · Joni Ernst is first woman from Iowa elected to serve in the United States Senate

2015 · Terry Branstad becomes longest serving governor in United States history, serving over 22 years

2017 · Kim Reynolds is first woman sworn in as governor of the state of Iowa

2018 · Cindy Axne and Abby Finkenauer are first women from Iowa elected to serve in the United States House of Representatives

2019 · 150th Anniversary of Terrace Hill

THE EXTERIOR

Terrace Hill is an exceptional example of the French Second Empire style. Use of the Second Empire style for domestic architecture became popular by the mid-1850s with examples built through the 1880s in various parts of the country. A steeply pitched mansard roof, multi-colored slate shingles, open verandas, dormer windows with elaborate surrounds and bracketed cornices are all part of this "Prairie Palace of the West." Prominent double door entrances face north, east and south. The brick house is trimmed in a combination of artificial stone, dressed limestone and ornamental wood millwork. Exterior walls are constructed with locally manufactured brick, and the quoins are made from artificial stone. Today, Terrace Hill represents a pure, minimally altered Second Empire building constructed for domestic use at the height of its style in the United States.

◀ South Façade

North Exterior, 1899

North Exterior, Present Day

NORTH EXTERIOR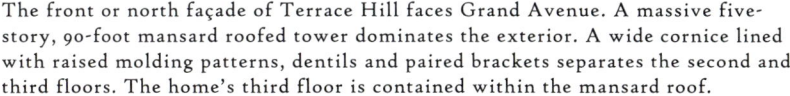

The front or north façade of Terrace Hill faces Grand Avenue. A massive five-story, 90-foot mansard roofed tower dominates the exterior. A wide cornice lined with raised molding patterns, dentils and paired brackets separates the second and third floors. The home's third floor is contained within the mansard roof.

East Exterior, 1899

East Exterior, Present Day

EAST EXTERIOR

The east façade of Terrace Hill looks out over a terraced hillside toward downtown Des Moines, with a view of the restored reflecting pool. A prominent four-story mansard roofed tower is set in the recessed ell. A richly ornamented porch spans the full width of the east side.

South Exterior, 1899

South Exterior, Present Day

SOUTH EXTERIOR

Terrace Hill's south façade looks out over the home's ornamental gardens and the Raccoon River Valley. The beautiful stained glass window is located directly above the portico. The mansard roof is clad in two colors of slate (red and brown) cut in four shapes (square, lancet, five-sided and six-sided) and laid in a diamond pattern.

West Exterior, 1899

West Exterior, Present Day

WEST EXTERIOR

The windows and doorway in the recessed center section have been altered on several occasions. Today, a private porch and entrance for the governor's family were modeled after the home's south entrance. Decorative wood-carved rope molding surrounds the doors and windows.

THE INTERIOR

Terrace Hill's interior displays a rich variety of ornamentation and finishes. Stenciled walls and ceilings, decorative plasterwork, a grand central staircase, elaborate fireplaces, an extraordinary stained glass window, finely crafted wood trim and casework and a fine collection of original light fixtures form a backdrop associated with the lives of the Allen and Hubbell families. Ceiling heights throughout the first floor are 15 feet, on the second floor they are 12 feet, and the ceiling height on the third floor is 9 feet. Wood floors in the main corridors are predominantly oak with walnut, cherry and maple added to create various patterns. Wood trim and doors use combinations of walnut, butternut, cherry, Colombian rosewood and oak. Each of the eight marble fireplaces in Terrace Hill has a unique design. The picturesque, asymmetrical design of Terrace Hill's exterior is reflected in the interior floor plan and finishes.

◄ North Tower Staircase

Drawing Room, 1913

Drawing Room, Present Day

DRAWING ROOM

Deceptively large (30 feet by 17 feet), the drawing room is the most formal room in the house. The fireplace mantel is made of white Italian marble, and the rosewood mirror over the mantel was manufactured by Jacob Ziegler, a New York City cabinet maker. The silver plated, lead crystal chandelier was installed by F.M. Hubbell. The 7 ½ foot high chandelier is thought to be Czechoslovakian and contains 2,213 individual pieces of glass crystal.

Reception Room, 1899

Reception Room, Present Day

RECEPTION ROOM

This room was originally the library when the Allen family lived in the house. F. M. Hubbell moved the library to its current location and created a reception room for visitors. The fireplace, one of two pink Spanish marble fireplaces original to the home, has a walnut mantel. The mirror above the mantel is eight feet tall and was manufactured by Jacob Ziegler of New York City. The doors, ceilings, paneling and trim in the reception room are a combination of walnut and butternut for contrasting effect.

Music Room, 1913

Music Room, Present Day

MUSIC ROOM

The tete-a-tete (French for head-to-head), or courting sofa, first became popular in the 19th century. It allowed courting couples to sit face-to-face, but also kept them from sitting too close to one another. This piece belonged to the Hubbell family and is seen in both photographs. The piano is an 1893 Steinway "Music Room Grand," autographed in 1986 by John Steinway and Iowa's own Roger Williams.

Dining Room, 1913

Dining Room, Present Day

DINING ROOM

F.M. Hubbell added the white oak wainscoting throughout the room as well as the sideboard on the north wall. All have hand-carved patterns of wheat, sunflowers and grape leaves. The chandelier was previously located in the music room and was moved into the dining room circa 1924. The mirror over the fireplace is nine feet tall and was installed by Grover Hubbell in the 1920s according to written dates found behind the mirror.

Main Hall, 1899

Main Hall, Present Day

MAIN HALL

The main hall is 10 feet wide, and the ceilings are 15 feet high. Arched openings spring from ornamental brackets that divide the ceiling. The arches create a dramatic visual effect, framing the view of the grand staircase at the opposite end of the main hall. Hinged double doors constructed of walnut with silver plate hardware fill the semicircular arched openings that open into the drawing room, reception room and music room.

East Hall, 1913

EAST HALL

East Hall, Present Day

The east hall extends from the east porch tower to the main hall. The original bronze light fixture, with rose colored globes, matches the two light fixtures in the main hall. The light fixtures were originally lit by gas and were converted to electricity in 1924. An elk mount and a caribou mount hang in the east hall. They were shot by Frederick Cooper Hubbell in Alaska.

35

Sitting Room, 1913

SITTING ROOM

Nearly as large as the drawing room, the sitting room served as the private family room. A grape leaf motif decorates the marble fireplace, and the mantel mirror is another Ziegler piece. The Turkish pierce-work brass chandelier is original to the room.

Sitting Room, Present Day

Library, 1899

LIBRARY

Library, Present Day

This room served as a billiards room when Allen lived at Terrace Hill but was made into the library when F.M. Hubbell moved into the home in 1884. F.M. Hubbell installed the walnut bookcases along the east and west walls. On the bookcase in the 1899 photograph, there is a three-piece Spelter clock set that is still on display today. The bronze and brass chandelier contains a pierce-work pattern on the center globe with opalescent glass jeweled inserts. Pocket doors set in a semicircular arched opening connect the library to the adjacent sitting room.

Grand Staircase, 1913

Grand Staircase, Present Day

GRAND STAIRCASE

The staircase is built in two flights. The first rises to a height of approximately 10 feet where a wide landing extends along the full width of the hallway. Separate return flights continue ascending to the second floor along the outer walls. The staircase has an elaborate balustrade fabricated of Colombian rosewood, walnut and oak. The newel post lights match the hall fixtures with rose colored globes and a bronze finish. Frederick Cooper Hubbell shot the moose that hangs at the bottom of the staircase.

41

Northwest Bedroom, 1899

Governor's Office, Present Day

NORTHWEST BEDROOM

Originally a bedroom, this room presently serves as the governor's home office. The white marble fireplace and mirror are original. The black horsehair-covered furniture belonged to Governor Samuel Kirkwood, who served as the fifth and the ninth governor of Iowa.

Northeast Bedroom, 1899

Northeast Bedroom, Present Day

NORTHEAST BEDROOM

The brass bed in this bedroom belonged to Beulah Hubbell, the daughter of F. M. Hubbell. Since Terrace Hill became the home of the governor, this bedroom serves as a guest room for visitors.

Southwest Bedroom Suite, Present Day

46

Southwest Bedroom, Present Day

SOUTHWEST BEDROOM

This room has views of the south garden, the river valley and the carriage house. Today, this room is used for visiting guests. The fireplace and mirror are original, and the bed belonged to F. M. Hubbell. The ensuite bathroom features period fixtures.

Southeast Bedroom, 1899

First Spouse Office Suite, Present Day

SOUTHEAST BEDROOM

This room is part of a suite that consists of an outer room, a bed chamber and a bathroom. These rooms have served various purposes over the years including a nursery and family sitting room. Today, this suite of rooms serves as an office for the first spouse.

Third Floor Kitchen, Present Day

Third Floor Living Room, Present Day

THIRD FLOOR RESIDENCE

The third floor originally housed residential quarters for Terrace Hill's household servants. In the 1970s, the third floor was remodeled to provide a home for Iowa's governor and family. The north tower contains a staircase that leads from the third floor to the fourth floor observation room.

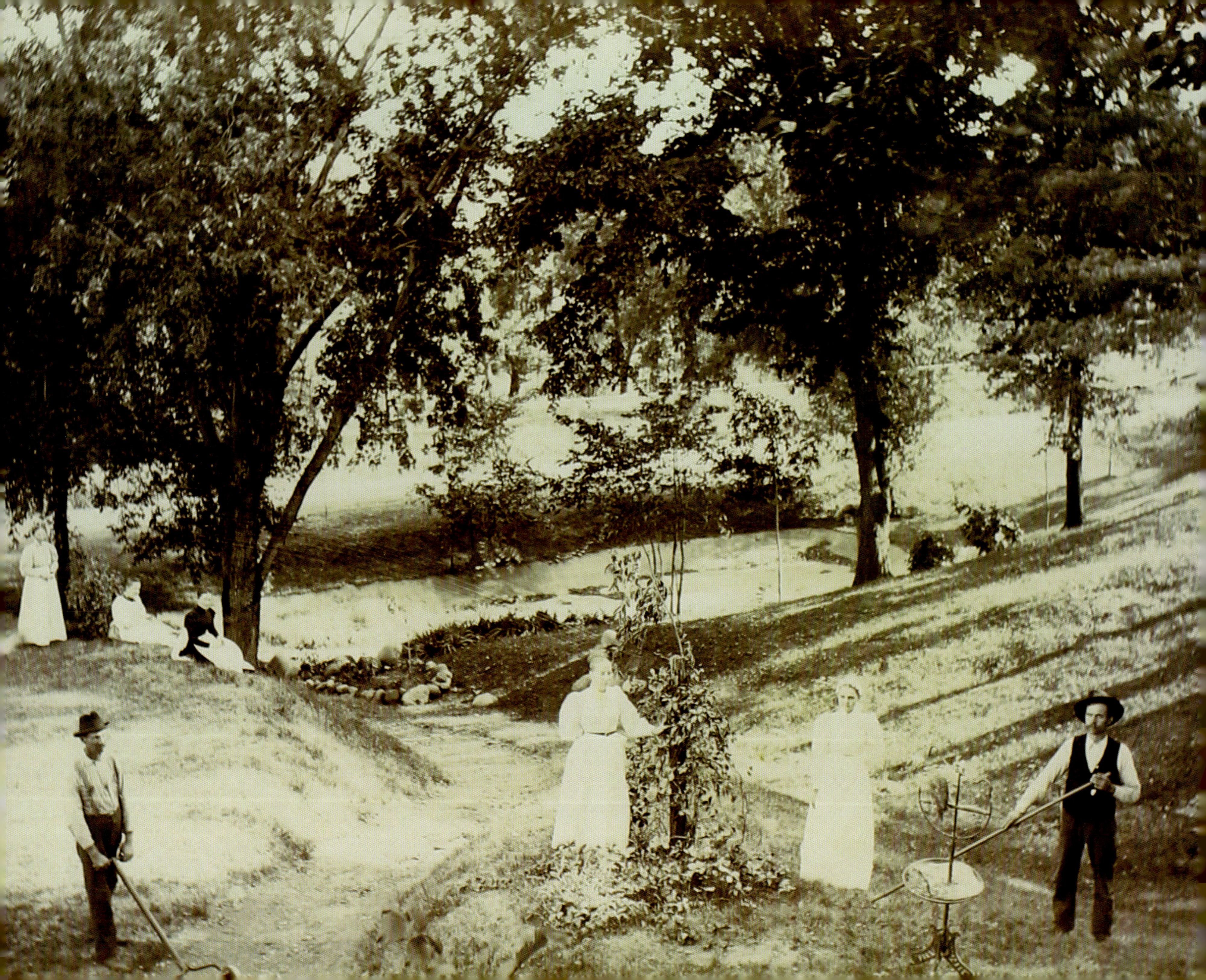

THE GROUNDS

When constructed at the end of the Civil War, Terrace Hill was located on the western outskirts of Des Moines overlooking the tree covered banks of the meandering east-west course of the Raccoon River. The photograph on the opposite page, taken in 1899, shows Terrace Hill servants, with their parrot, working near a pond on the southeastern boundary of the property. The original site contained 29 acres and the present parcel contains eight acres. The Terrace Hill site contains a mix of plant materials. Most of the grounds are manicured lawns with a mix of deciduous and coniferous trees. Between 1964 and 1969, approximately 100 diseased American elm trees were removed and replaced with 10 different varieties of trees. In 2017, a study conducted by the Iowa State University Community Design Lab identified 221 trees representing 53 species.

◀ Southeast Grounds, 1899

Pool, 1937

Pool, Present Day

POOL

The pool, added to the site in 1928 by Grover Hubbell, was one of the first private swimming pools in Des Moines. It measured 60 feet long by 21 feet wide and 10 feet at its greatest depth. At the south end of the pool, a stone arbor with a U-shaped footprint was built. A vine covered, wood pergola served as the roof. The stone walls remain in place today. Circa 1990, the pool was filled in and covered with grass. In 2016, the pool was excavated and a 16-inch-deep reflecting pool was constructed in the original footprint.

Carriage House, 1899

Carriage House, Present Day

CARRIAGE HOUSE

The brick carriage house is located on a rise along the west edge of the property. Substantial portions of the building date from 1866 to 1869, the construction period of the house. Originally, the carriage house had a mansard roof to match the residence. A major roof alteration prior to 1901 created the present appearance of the building. Today, the carriage house contains a visitor's center, a gift shop, administrative offices and a maintenance shop. The area that serves as a gift shop was initially the ice house.

East Lawn Garden Bed, 1899

GARDENS

On the lawn east of the porch, a multi-lobed garden is planted with annuals, mimicking a flower bed that existed in 1899. Historic photographs provided inspiration for much of the current landscape.

East Lawn Garden Bed, Present Day

South Entry Garden, 1899

South Entry Garden, Present Day

GARDENS

The south side of the house is ideal for a garden bed. Cannas lined the sidewalk in 1899 and they are still part of the present-day landscape.

South Garden, 1899

South Garden, Present Day

GARDENS

In 1899, the south garden was the site for a greenhouse which served the house and the grounds. The current south garden was installed in the 1980s and consists of raised beds for vegetables, a shade garden and a perennial border. The present-day garden pergola, built in 2005, replicates a pergola that existed in this garden during the late 1920s.

THE FUTURE OF TERRACE HILL

In addition to serving as the home of Iowa's governor and first family, Terrace Hill is one of the outstanding house museums in America. Each year brings thousands of visitors from across the nation and around the world.

The extraordinary past of this landmark is indeed prologue for the future. In 2019, Terrace Hill celebrated 150 years of existence as one of Iowa's - and America's - finest treasures, and the story is not finished. Each governor that takes up residence, each project that restores the property more closely to its original condition and each visitor that passes through its halls is a part of Terrace Hill's history and its continually unfolding future. Today, Terrace Hill is alive as an influential piece of history preserved for future generations of Iowans to experience, learn from and enjoy.

◀ Front Entry

ISBN — 978-0-9983128-5-9

Published by   Heuss Printing   Photography by   Gary Hoard Photography
                 903 North 2nd Street
                 Ames, Iowa 50010

First edition published 2019. All rights reserved. No part of this publication may be reproduced, stored in a retrieval system, or transmitted in any form, electronic, mechanical, photocopying, recording or scanning or otherwise, except as permitted under Section 107 or 108 of the 1976 United States Copyright Act, without the express written permission of the publisher and author. Requests to the publisher for permission should be addressed to the Permissions Department, Heuss Printing, 903 North Second Street, Ames, Iowa 50010. (800) 232.6710.

South Lawn, Present Day ▶